BILLY JOEL

by Robbie Gennet & Todd Lowry

The Recording

The accompanying audio includes full-band demos with featured keyboard parts isolated on the right side of the stereo mix. Keyboard parts that warrant closer attention are played alone as slow demos where shown.

Warren Wiegratz: Keyboards and Saxophone
Doug Boduch: Guitars
Tom McGirr: Bass
Scott Schroedl: Drums

PLAYBACK+
Speed • Pitch • Balance • Loop

To access audio visit:
www.halleonard.com/mylibrary

"Enter Code"
6446-1988-8978-5843

Cover photo by Neal Preston/CORBIS

ISBN 978-1-5400-9181-9

Visit Hal Leonard Online at
www.halleonard.com

Contact us:
Hal Leonard
7777 West Bluemound Road
Milwaukee, WI 53213
Email: info@halleonard.com

In Europe, contact:
Hal Leonard Europe Limited
42 Wigmore Street
Marylebone, London, W1U 2RN
Email: info@halleonardeurope.com

In Australia, contact:
Hal Leonard Australia Pty. Ltd.
4 Lentara Court
Cheltenham, Victoria, 3192 Australia
Email: info@halleonard.com.au

CONTENTS

Page

INTRODUCTION
Billy Joel: A Brief Biography

Billy Joel is a classically trained pop composer who has many multi-platinum records and hit singles to his name. His songs have struck a chord with a widespread audience of all ages, and New Yorkers in particular have latched on to his localized characters and stories. This book/audio package will break down some of the most memorable moments of his work from the early 1970s to early 1990s, a period of great creativity during which he produced some of his most timeless and successful songs.

William Martin Joel was born on May 9, 1949 in Bronx, NY. While he was a young child, his family moved to Levittown on Long Island. Joel discovered classical music at the age of four, and this love has been with him to the present. His father, a German-born engineer, was enthused about young Billy's interest in Mozart, and started him on classical piano lessons, which would continue for ten years. Joel's early classical training provided him with a strong foundation for his career.

Among Joel's early influences were Ray Charles, The Beatles, Dave Brubeck, Sam Cooke, the Rolling Stones, and Otis Redding. His ambition to become a professional musician began when he saw the Beatles perform on the Ed Sullivan Show in 1964. At age fourteen, Joel joined his first band, the Echoes (later known as the Lost Souls). The band played for parties and school events.

Joel also became a professional session player in his teens, working with George "Shadow" Morton. His most notable session of that time was on "Leader of the Pack" by the Shangri-La's. He also performed with a string of original bands and eventually dropped out of high school to concentrate on his budding musical career. After a few records with his band the Hassles, Joel regrouped a duo under the name Attila, playing a heavy, organ-based brand of psychedelic rock—a far cry from the music for which he would come to be known. Signed to Epic Records, Attila didn't find the success Joel had hoped for, and he fell into depression. After a few years, Billy signed a new record deal and released his solo debut, 1971's *Cold Spring Harbor*. Though his tour was well received, he was unhappy with the record and having trouble with his label. In 1972, he moved to Los Angeles and spent most of the year playing lounge piano under the name Bill Martin.

By the beginning of 1973, Joel had married his long-time girlfriend and was touring again. During this time, a Philadelphia radio station started playing a live version of "Captain Jack," and suddenly record labels were knocking on his door. After signing with Columbia, he recorded and released his major-label debut, *Piano Man*, which peaked the following year at #27 on the Billboard 200 album chart and garnered his first Top 40 hit with the title track, an ode to his time spent in the piano bar. His second album, *Streetlife Serenade*, reached the Top 40 as well and featured songs such as "The Entertainer" and "Root Beer Rag." In the midst of his rising popularity (and the first batch of many music industry awards to come), his growing dissatisfaction with California found him moving back east to his true hometown, New York City.

With new management on board, Joel released the self-produced *Turnstiles* in 1976, featuring the semi-autobiographical "Say Goodbye to Hollywood" and his paean to the Big Apple, "New York State of Mind." Though *Turnstiles* didn't fare well commercially, Joel was honing his craft as a songwriter and was about to unleash his biggest album yet. He teamed up with legendary producer Phil Ramone and released *The Stranger* in the fall of 1977. Within months, it went to #2 and sold millions. Besides the classic ballad "Just the Way You Are"—Record and Song of the Year at the 1979 GRAMMYs—the album also featured the Top 20 hits "Movin' Out (Anthony's Song)," "She's Always a Woman," and "Only the Good Die Young." Joel enlisted Ramone again for the follow-up album, *52nd Street*.

Released in the fall of 1978, it spent eight weeks at #1 in the U.S. and sold over two million copies within a month of its release. *52nd Street* won GRAMMYs for Album of the Year and Best Male Pop Vocal Performance in 1980, while pop radio made hits of "My Life," "Big Shot," and "Honesty." Joel was not always the critics' darling, but his legions of fans and multi-platinum record sales more than made up for it. In fact, in 1979 Columbia Records named him their biggest-selling solo artist of the 20th century, with sales of *The Stranger* and *52nd Street* then totaling over nine million units.

Joel followed the two hit records with his hardest-rocking album yet, the punk- and new wave-tinged *Glass Houses*, released in 1980. It would go on to reach #1 and stay there for six weeks, winning a GRAMMY for Best Rock Vocal Performance, as well as an American Music Award for Album of the Year and the People's Choice Favorite Male Pop Performer. "It's Still Rock 'n' Roll to Me" was Joel's first #1 hit and his biggest single to date. "You May Be Right," "Don't Ask Me Why," and "Sometimes a Fantasy" all hit the Top 40 as well. He followed up *Glass Houses* with his first live record, *Songs in the Attic*, which focused solely on earlier material. Live versions of "Say Goodbye to Hollywood" and "She's Got a Way" became Top 40 hits, and *Songs in the Attic* became Billy's fourth consecutive Top 10 album.

Soon after *Songs in the Attic* was released, Joel suffered a broken wrist in a motorcycle accident and went through a painful divorce. His next album, *The Nylon Curtain*, didn't sell as well as its predecessors, though critics were warming up to him. Big radio hits like "Pressure" and "Allentown" were featured on the newly blossomed MTV. *An Innocent Man* soon followed, reaching #4 in 1983. Nominated for the Album of the Year GRAMMY, it generated six Top 40 singles, including three that reached the Top 10: "Uptown Girl" (#3), "Tell Her About It" (#1), and "An Innocent Man" (#10). By 1985, Joel had enough hits to fill a two-volume Greatest Hits collection featuring two new singles: "You're Only Human (Second Wind)"—his eighth Top 10 hit—and "The Night Is Still Young." Greatest Hits sold over 20 million copies in the U.S. alone, cementing Joel's status as a pop icon.

Billy's next album of new music was *The Bridge*, which made the Top 10 in 1986, spawning the hits "Modern Woman," "A Matter of Trust," and "This Is the Time." Ray Charles, Steve Winwood, and Cyndi Lauper all appeared on the album in a rare spate of guest spots. Joel then became one of the first Western artists to tour the USSR, recording his 1987 Leningrad performance for the live album *Kohuept* (Russian for "concert"). The next original album was his 14th for Columbia, the multi-platinum *Storm Front*, released in 1989. The #1 hit "We Didn't Start the Fire" was used in schools nationwide as a learning tool due to its fact-based historical lyrics. *Storm Front* reached #1, received numerous GRAMMY nominations, and also produced the hits "I Go to Extremes" and "Shameless" (which was very successfully covered by Garth Brooks). In 1990, the National Academy of Recording Arts and Sciences honored Billy Joel with a GRAMMY Living Legend award. After a four-year recording hiatus, Joel released *River of Dreams* in 1993. The album quickly reached #1, and the title track was a Top 10 hit. Four GRAMMY nominations followed in 1994, as well as certification that *Songs in the Attic* and *The Nylon Curtain* had hit the two million in sales mark—moving Joel into a tie with the Beatles as the act with the most multi-platinum albums. Joel also became the only artist to have four albums—*52nd Street*, *Glass Houses*, *The Stranger*, and *An Innocent Man*—go septuple-platinum. In March 1997, Joel received ASCAP's Founder's Award for lifetime achievement—joining the ranks of Paul McCartney, Bob Dylan, Leiber and Stoller, and other music legends. With worldwide sales of over 100 million units by 1999, Joel marked two more music milestones: in January he received the American Music Awards' Award of Merit, and in February he was inducted into the Rock and Roll Hall of Fame. In May of 2000 he was awarded an honorary Doctor of Music from Southampton College—one of many honorary degrees he has received.

River of Dreams was the last pop album Billy Joel released. Since then, he has put out the live *2000 Years: The Millennium Concert* and 2001's classical endeavor *Fantasies and Delusions*. Both were well received by fans, who also flocked to the Elton John/Billy Joel concert tours the two had undertaken. In 2001, Joel was honored by the Songwriter's Hall of Fame with the Johnny Mercer Award—their highest honor.

Billy Joel is a top-notch song craftsman with a great ear for memorable hooks. His primary instrument is the acoustic piano, but he has also played electric piano, Hammond B-3 organ, and an array of synthesizers on albums. Joel's keyboard parts range from sensitive acoustic piano on ballads such as "She's Got a Way" to raucous, pounding rock piano on "I Go to Extremes." His keyboard parts incorporate blues riffs ("Baby Grand"), elements of 1960s Rhythm & Blues ("Tell Her About It"), and classical touches ("And So It Goes"), among many other influences. Joel's classical foundation is clearly evident in his strong knowledge of harmony, frequently incorporating extended chords, slash chords, inversions, add9 chords, and altered dominants. His songs are usually very adventurous harmonically.

Joel has been a longtime supporter of the Make a Wish Foundation (www.wish. org) and VH1's *Save the Music Foundation* (www.savethemusic.org).

Billy Joel is one of the great musical artists of the last 40-plus years. His music is certain to be around for generations to come, alongside that of such artists as Lennon and McCartney, Elton John, and Stevie Wonder. Hopefully, this book will contribute to the appreciation of his genius.

ALL ABOUT SOUL

Words and Music by Billy Joel
From the album _The River of Dreams,_ released in 1993.

"All About Soul" is a love song with a big beat and a huge "wall-of-sound" production. Joel is credited in the album notes with playing acoustic piano and Hammond organ. However, the organ sound cannot be heard distinctly in the wall of sound created by the power chords and large vocal ensemble, and therefore is not reproduced here.

Figure 1 – Intro/Verse/Chorus

The intro features a Dsus2 chord (D, E, and A) resolving to a D minor chord and an E♭sus2 chord (E♭, F, and B♭) resolving to E♭ major. The piano part in the verse is about as simple as it gets. Chords in the right hand and bass notes in octaves in the left hand are sustained for four beats in conjunction with the heavily processed electric guitar power chords. Note the use of various chord _inversions_ in the chorus—C/E, B♭/D, F/C, C/B♭, etc. (A chord inversion has a chord tone other than the root in the bass.) Joel often uses inversions to spice up a chord progression and to make the bass line more interesting.

1 Full Band

2 Slow Demo
Piano meas. 1-4

Fig. 1

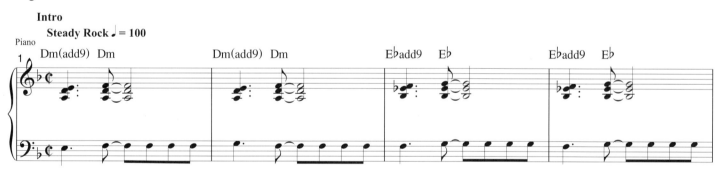

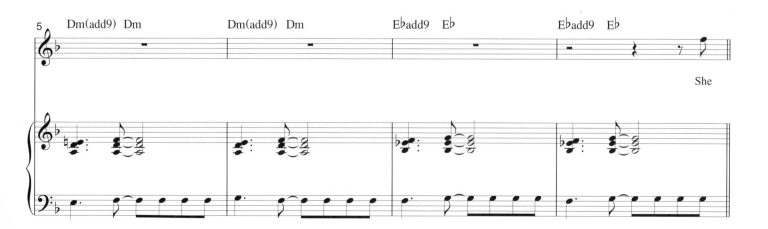

AND SO IT GOES

Words and Music by Billy Joel
From the album _Storm Front,_ released in 1989.

In many of Billy Joel's love songs, there is an underlying somber tone, a sense of insecurity or a fear of abandonment. "And So It Goes" has that tone—"And so it goes, and so it goes/And so will you soon I suppose." For Joel, love has a potentially sad side—"You can have my heart to break."

The music to "And So It Goes," however, is quite beautiful. It's a very slow waltz with a slightly weary lilt and plenty of _rubato_. This means that the music is played with freedom regarding tempo; i.e., the music is played "with feeling" and not necessarily with a strict beat.

This piece could be considered a predecessor to Joel's later classical compositions. The chords, which change on nearly every melodic note, seem very classical in nature.

Figure 2 – Intro/Verse 1/Verse 2/Bridge/Verse 3

The song makes generous use of chord inversions and added 9th chords. Note especially the voicings of the Cmaj7/E and Fadd9 chords in the first two measures. Joel knows how to take a standard chord and voice it for a rich and colorful sonority. The bridge features a chromatically descending bass line beginning at measure 25.

Fig. 2

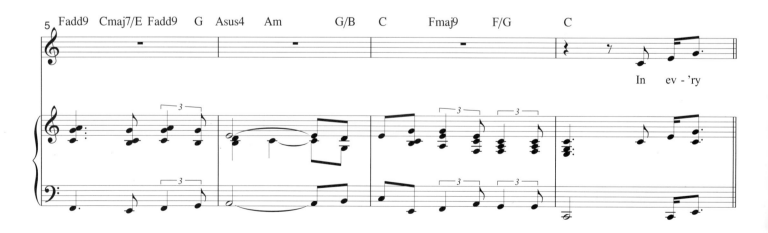

* Synthesizer pad doubles piano part.

BIG SHOT

Words and Music by Billy Joel
From the album *52nd Street,* released in 1978.

In one of Billy Joel's most vicious songs, he cuts down a NYC socialite who evidently made a fool of herself while under the influence. Joel's scathing commentary on the jet-set crowd rings true as he tells the "big shot" in question about her embarrassing behavior at some uptown party the night before, and rips into her for going "over the line" and making a fool of herself. This is a classic Joel hit, and his sneering vocals deliver the song's message perfectly.

Figure 3—Intro and Verse 1

"Big Shot" is in the key of C major, but it starts out feeling very much like E minor due to the way the chords are used. Notice that the intro begins in bass clef, as the low piano doubles the classic guitar riff that starts the song. The first four measures go through the Em7sus–G riff twice, with hits on the "and" of beats 1 and 3 in measure 4. The Bm chord (over a D bass note) in measure 6 works very well as a link from Em to C.

A repeated Em(sus) chord in measure 8 leads into the verse, which continues along the same basic chord progression as the intro. Notice how the notes D and A are suspended throughout the dark verse chords, until the release on measures 15–16 with the C and F/C.

Fig. 3

Figure 4—Chorus

Again, a repeated eighth-note chord—this time G major—sets up the chorus. The chorus chords are diatonic, from the C major scale, and stick with the IV, V, and vi (F, G, and Am). The bass line in the left hand, however, is on a different track melodically and rhythmically, and its movement gives the song impetus. In the first four measures, Joel sticks to F and C in the bass, using them in relation to the G and F chords on top to create a Lydian-type sound. In measures 6–8, the bass line moves up a whole step to G and D, similarly bouncing back and forth below the same chords on top and brightening things up in the process. Transitional C–E bass-note punches in measure 9 lead back into the cycle, until the big release in measures 14–17, a legato chord movement setting up the return to the intro riff.

Fig. 4

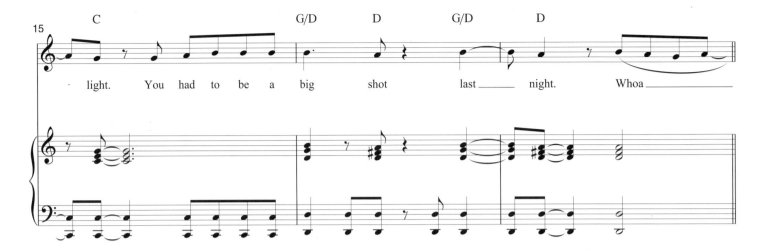

Figure 5—Bridge

The second time through the chorus leads to the bridge. The bass notes arpeggiate the notes of the chords above them, such as F–A–C under the F chord in measure 1. When one writes on piano, those climbing left-hand octaves are very natural, especially in rock 'n' roll. The main chords follow a "cycle of fifths" progression pounded in straight eighths: F–C–G–D.

6 Full Band

7 Slow Demo: meas. 1-4

Fig. 5

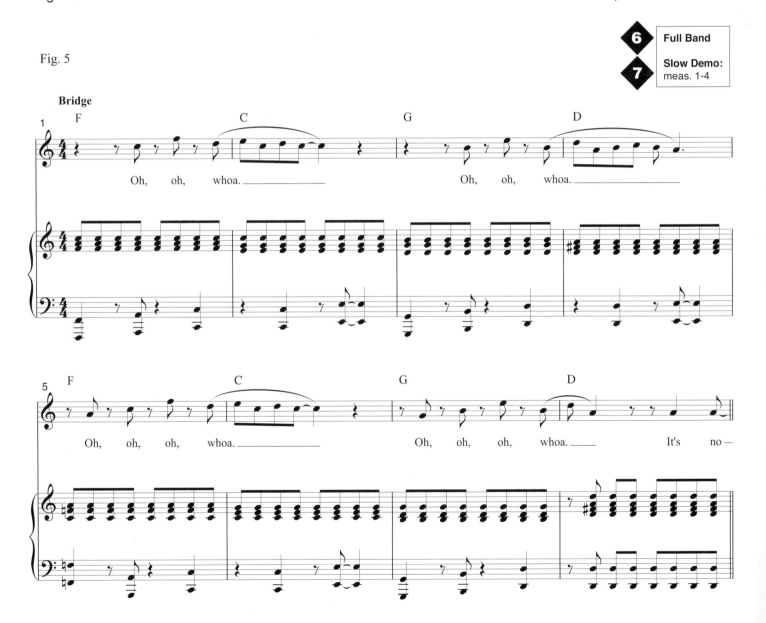

CAPTAIN JACK

Words and Music by Billy Joel
From the album *Piano Man,* released in 1973.

"Captain Jack" is an early Billy Joel narrative about a teenage loner living on the fringes of New York City. Joel captures the essence of a young man with too much time on his hands and no clear idea of his future, placing the lyrics in the second person so the listener becomes the subject. "Captain Jack" is either a drug or the dealer who brings it, and the artificial escape from a "one-horse town" never fills the emptiness inside. The protagonist has "everything"—cool clothes, a brand new car, a girlfriend—yet is never satisfied, and he tries to fill his hollow heart with drugs and seedy hangouts. But ultimately, though he hasn't found the answers to his emptiness, he sees it all coming to an end in the line, "Well, you're twenty-one and still your mother makes your bed, and that's too long." Joel's story is one to which most people can relate: the feeling that in our teen years, nobody truly understands us because in reality, we don't understand ourselves. "Captain Jack" is a timeless story that resonates decades after its inception. As long as there are teenagers struggling with self-discovery, "Captain Jack" will remain a poignant story and song.

Figure 6—Intro

The first two measures of the intro (played on pipe organ) are comprised of a 16th-note figure in the right hand and a simple line in the left that implies the noted chord structure in the key of G. (This brief statement in G might seem odd now, but Joel is foreshadowing the chorus.) The C chord in measure 2 acts as a *pivot chord* (a chord present in two keys): the IV in G, and the V in F. When the piano enters in measure 3, he oscillates between the I and IV chords (F and B♭).

8 **Full Band**

9 **Slow Demo:** meas. 1-2

Fig. 6

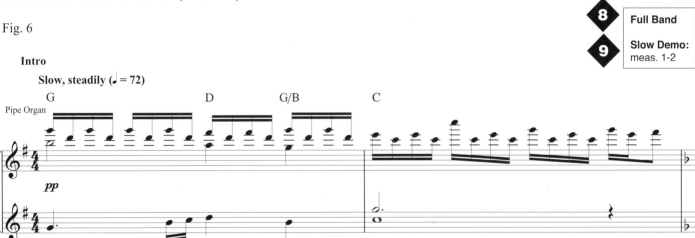

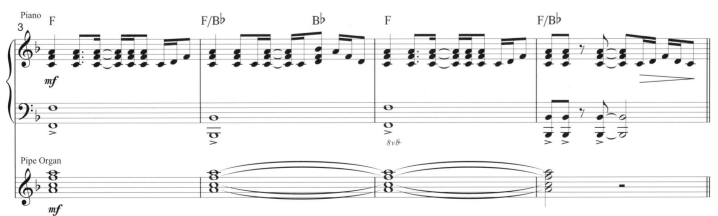

Figure 7—Verse

In the first five measures of the verse, Joel continues the I–IV–I movement. He uses a B♭maj7 the first two times, then switches up the change with a transitory Bm7♭5 to an unadorned B♭ chord in measure 6. He then drops from the IV chord (B♭) to the iii7 chord (Am7), and then moves to the V chord (C) to set up the return to the I chord (F). The next eight-measure verse works much the same, with two notable exceptions: first, Joel discards the Bm7♭5 for a simpler B♭(add9) in the third line; second, in the last bar, he moves from the Am to a D, a setup for the key change to G major in the chorus. Keep in mind that Am–D–G is a ii–V–I progression in G Major, a strong progression that works well in a transitional section.

Fig. 7

Figure 8—Chorus

The chorus is comprised mostly of the I, IV, and V chords in G major. Notice at the end of measure 1 how Joel uses the G with the 3rd in the bass (G/B) to lead into the C chord, a common technique in his bag of tricks and an effective way to generate motion in a progression.

Fig. 8

11 Full Band

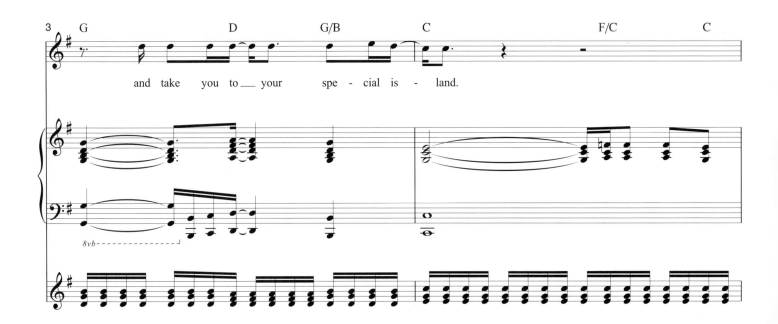

Cap - tain Jack __ will get you by __ to - night, __

just a lit - tle push 'n' you'll be smil - in'. __

THE ENTERTAINER

Words and Music by Billy Joel
From the album _Streetlife Serenade,_ released in 1974.

In "The Entertainer," Joel tells of the highs and lows of being in show business. He traces the steps in rising to fame, but leads to the fact that without a hit, you can quickly disappear. No matter what the genre or decade, the sentiments Joel expresses ring true in an increasingly corporate game that often depends on expendable artists and ever-changing trends. The song's epic feel and complex arrangements seem to defy the corporate music scene.

Figure 9—Intro

"The Entertainer" begins with this bright, syncopated melodic statement played on synth above a sprightly strummed acoustic guitar part. The piano plays a closely related part with simple harmonies in G. The synth is played with a slight portamento or "glide" setting to make each note slide into the next.

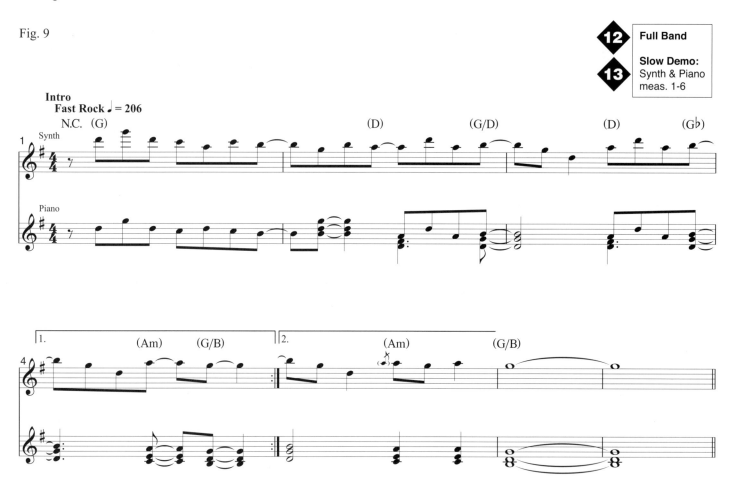

Figure 10—Verse 3 and Interlude

Joel accompanies his voice on piano only in certain verses. The third verse is the first and simplest appearance of piano accompaniment—just full chords hit on the syncopated changes. The verse's construction begins with three symmetrical four-measure phrases, then a five-measure phrase added at the end, making a total of seventeen measures per verse (instead of the anticipated sixteen). The interlude is a synth/piano riff reminiscent of the intro.

Fig. 10

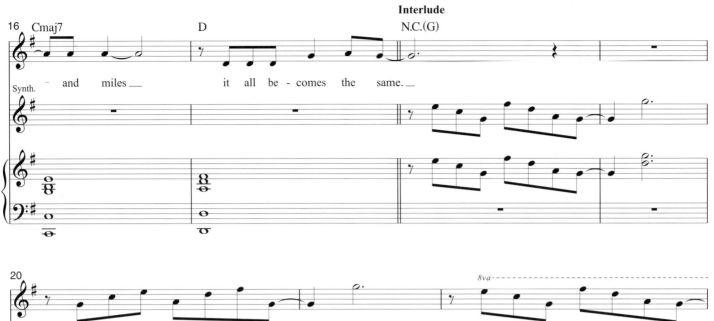

Figure 11—Verse 5

This is the most involved verse, pianistically speaking. The piano begins with a two-measure lead-in to the verse, and already shows the bluesy direction we're headed. Joel plays an invigorating boogie-woogie piano part that would sound like an all-out solo if not for the vocal.

Fig. 11

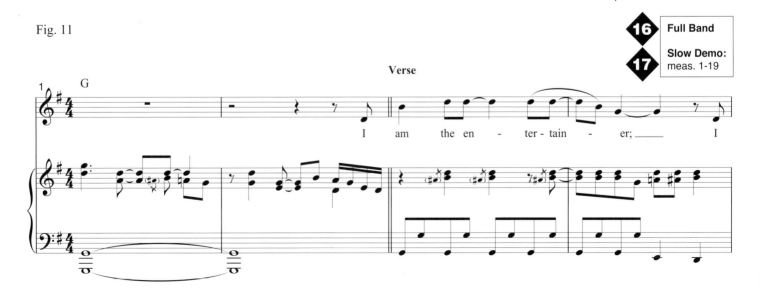

HONESTY

Words and Music by Billy Joel
From the album *52nd Street,* released in 1978.

"Honesty" is one of Joel's "moral of the story" songs, touching on a subject with which everyone struggles at some point or another. Joel switches back and forth from second to first person in his exploration of truth and communication, searching for sincerity from others while alluding to the false security that empty promises and sympathy bring only temporarily. In the chorus, he tells us that "everyone is so untrue," but that the honesty he really needs is not from everyone in the world, but from his lover. The song's delicate feel and descending and rising chord progressions mirror this sentiment.

Figure 12—Intro, Verse, and Chorus

"Honesty" is in B♭ Major, but Joel clearly begins in B♭ minor, only moving toward the major after the F7 is struck in measure 2. During the verse, he plays primarily diatonic chords in a simple quarter-note rhythm. Just before the chorus he plays a ii–V in G—only to resolve to E♭, a deceptive resolution that is sometimes heard in the key of G minor. In the chorus, Joel seems centered in G minor, partly due to the strong D/F♯–Gm resolutions, and also because of the prominent D7s (V of Gm), even though they invariably resolve deceptively to E♭.

Fig. 12

JUST THE WAY YOU ARE

Words and Music by Billy Joel
From the album _The Stranger,_ released in 1977.

One of the most endearing love songs of Billy Joel's career, "Just the Way You Are" is a classy ballad that deals directly with one of love's greatest features, acceptance. The famous opening line, "Don't go changing to try and please me," leads to the beautiful chorus sentiment "I love you just the way you are," as Joel gives reassurance that his love is heartfelt and everlasting. It is a true song of love, one dedicated at many weddings— and rightfully so. The song was a huge hit for Joel, and is now considered a standard. Its elegant arrangement, including a tasteful sax solo from jazz legend Phil Woods, rolls over a vaguely Latin groove.

Figure 13—Intro, Verse 1, and Verse 2

The heavily-chorused Rhodes electric piano that opens the song helps make this intro instantly recognizable. Joel cleverly alternates occurrences of the iv chord (Gm6) with the IV chord (G).

In the verse, Billy uses a variety of jazzy sixth and seventh chords, as well as many ii–V–I progressions (the archetypical jazz standard progression). The major-turning-minor sound of the Gmaj7–Gm7 movement in measures 9–10 harks back to the major/minor duality of the intro. The end of the second verse is slightly different from the first in terms of its harmony (Em7–G/A in meas. 33–34, instead of E9sus–E7–G/A in 17–19). Joel tacks on an ending (not shown) just after the title line that matches the intro.

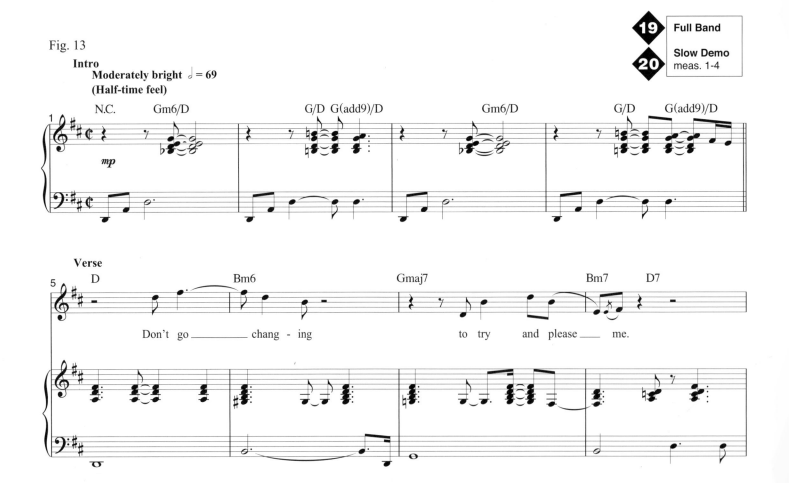

Fig. 13

19 Full Band
20 Slow Demo meas. 1-4

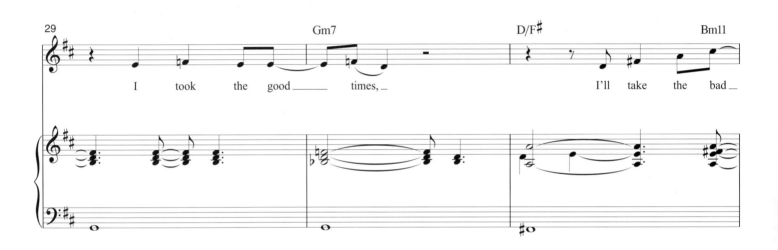

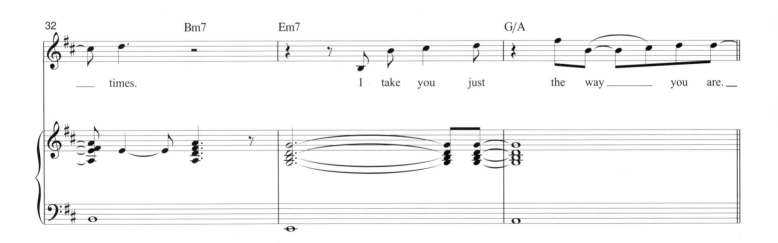

Figure 14—Bridge

The bridge is another fine example of the way Billy Joel effortlessly weaves his progressions in and out of different key areas. (Compare this to the bridge in "New York State of Mind.") Notice also how the chords embellish and complement the vocal: In measures 9–10, a descending C chord mirrors the descending vocal melody; in measures 15–16, Joel climbs up four positions of the G/A chord to fill in the break and set up the next verse.

Fig. 14

LENINGRAD

Words and Music by Billy Joel
From the album *Storm Front,* released in 1989.

In 1987, Billy Joel became the first American pop star to bring a fully-staged rock tour to the Soviet Union. "Leningrad" reflects the influence of that tour. The song tells the story of a young Russian man named Victor who grows up in post-war Russia, which is contrasted with Joel's own upbringing during the Cold War. At the song's conclusion, the two end up friends.

Figure 15 – Intro/Verse 1/Verse 2

This elegant, regal, march-like intro anticipates Billy Joel's later classical compositions. This piece sounds as if a post-Romantic composer could have written it.

In the intro, the chords change on nearly every melodic note, and Joel uses chord inversions very effectively. The verse features rolling *broken chords*—a sort of piano equivalent of a guitarist fingerpicking chords.

Fig. 15

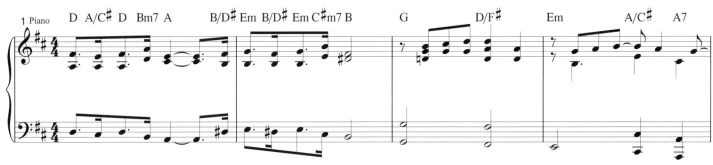

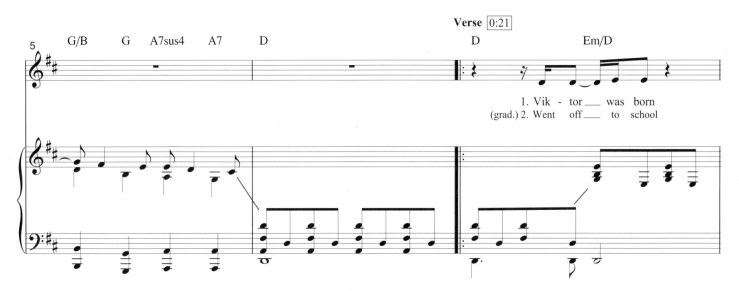

LULLABYE (GOODNIGHT, MY ANGEL)

Words and Music by Billy Joel
From the album *The River of Dreams,* released in 1993.

This tender, graceful lullabye is built on reassuring words from parent to child and a graceful acoustic piano part. Once again, this piece foreshadows Joel's later classical piano compositions.

Figure 16 – Intro/Verse

The intro and verse are based largely on both major and minor versions of the IV chord (i.e. C major and C minor) alternating with the G major tonic chord.

Fig. 16

Figure 17 – Interlude

The song, which began in G major, moves to G minor in the interlude, and the mood becomes somewhat darker.

Fig. 17

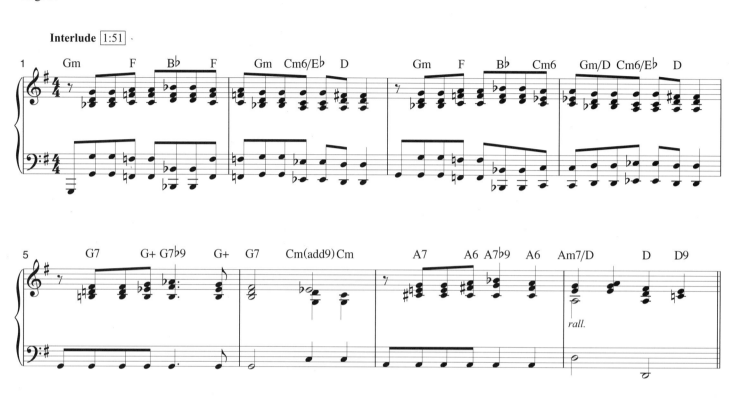

MOVIN' OUT (ANTHONY'S SONG)

Words and Music by Billy Joel
From the album *The Stranger,* released in 1977.

In another of Joel's story songs, the main character Anthony is leaving home, motorcycle screeching as he tears off in search of a better life. Though the verses are written in the third person, Joel puts himself in Anthony's shoes in the chorus, personalizing the disillusionment and escapism in Anthony's struggle for independence. What is Anthony escaping? The status quo of working and living in his ethnic neighborhood for a house and a car just like all his neighbors. He asks, "Is that all you get for your money?" and follows with "It seems such a waste of time if that's what it's all about." Anthony's search for greater meaning in life is shared by most people transitioning from young, carefree teenagers into responsible adults, and the liberating roar of his motorcycle signifies a powerful—if temporary—escape from a "normal" life.

Figure 18—Intro

The song starts out with simple right-hand chords played in steady eighths on piano, as the bass line, doubled by a lightly distorted guitar, gives contrasting rhythmic movement and leads us from chord to chord.

The song is in the key of D minor, and most of the chords are diatonic. The only chromatic exception in the intro is the E+, which Joel uses to link the C to the Fmaj7. The voice leading in the right hand is very smooth throughout, and the E+ makes it even more so.

Fig. 18

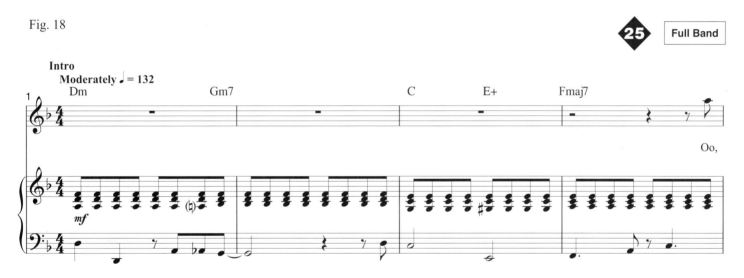

Figure 19—Verse and Pre-Chorus

The verse is based on the progression established in the intro, but Joel makes some slight changes: He substitutes a C9sus for the plain C, an E7♭9 instead of E+, and a plain F triad for the Fmaj7. However, they function in the same way, which is important to notice and is corroborated by the bass line, which is essentially unchanged.

In measure 10, Joel dispenses with the right hand's insistent eighth-note rhythms, and lays down a whole note chord under the "heart attack-ack-ack-ack-ack-ack" line, one of more recognizable parts in the song.

The pre-chorus (meas. 17–23) serves as a setup to the title line, and lasts an uneven seven measures. The half-time feel and the three-note descending guitar figures create a downward spiral of sound that reflects Joel's rejection of middle-class values. The following eight-measure chorus (not shown) is essentially the same as the verse, with added woodwind parts and octaves in the bass line.

Fig. 19

26 **Full Band**

27 **Slow Demo:** meas. 16

Figure 20—Outro

It is here that we hear the revving of Anthony's motorcycle as he tears off and moves out, and this starts a musical ending and eventual fade. Joel jumps to the key of D major, giving an uplifting finale to the piece. This extreme variation of the main chord pattern becomes a majestic outro, complete with harmony lead guitar lines that double the piano melody.

Fig. 20

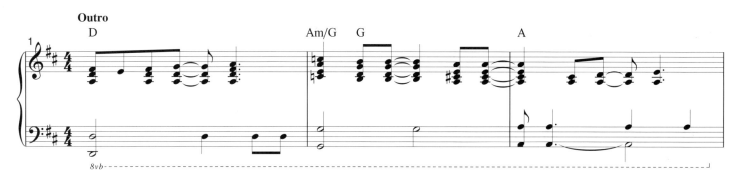

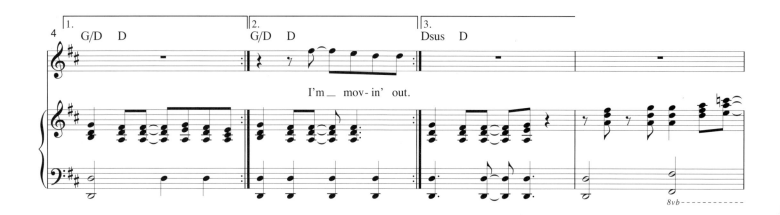

I'm__ mov- in' out.

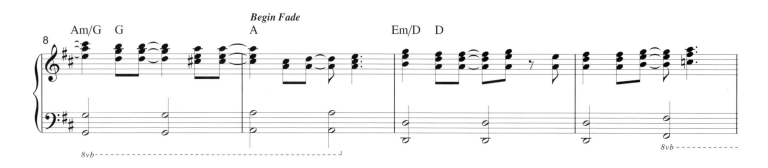

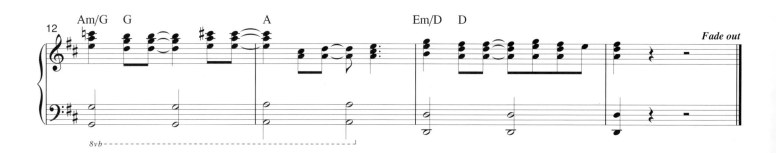

MY LIFE

Words and Music by Billy Joel
From the album *52nd Street,* released in 1978.

One of Billy Joel's biggest hits, the upbeat pop song "My Life" is a manifesto to independence, delivered succinctly with the chorus line "I don't care what you say anymore, this is my life. Go ahead with your own life. Leave me alone." This is a gentle kiss-off to parents, or perhaps a controlling lover, and Joel gets his point across without anger or negativity. Much of the song is written in the first person, as Joel speaks directly to his oppressor, using terms like "I don't want you to tell me..." or "I don't care what you say..." as he leads to the uncompromising "you can speak your mind, but not on my time." Surely many people were inspired by this song to stand for what they believe in, and discount the sometimes ill-stated opinions of others.

Figure 21—Intro, Interlude, and Verse

"My Life" begins with a grooving introduction consisting of simple chords over a D pedal point. But before long, Joel reaches outside the key for some added color, particularly during the interlude, where nearly all the chords are borrowed—D9, C9, E♭maj7/F, F7, and B♭.

Joel uses a chromatic, disco-style (no one was really immune to disco fever in '78) walk-up in measure 16 to set up the verse, which is firmly rooted back in D major.

Fig. 21

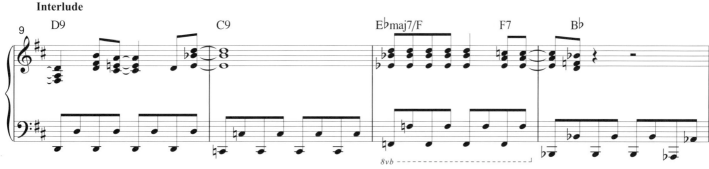

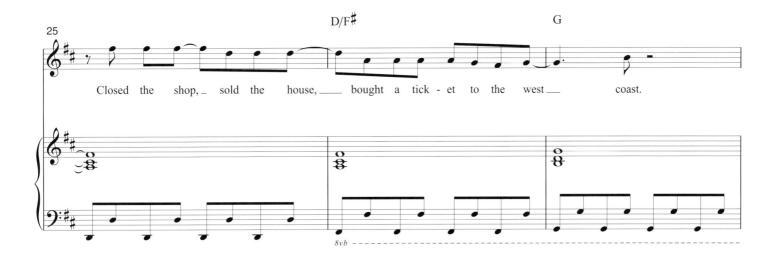

Closed the shop,_ sold the house,___ bought a tick - et to the west___ coast.

Now, he gives_ them a stand - up rou - tine_ in L. A._

Figure 22—Bridge

After a chorus that is identical to the verse, the bridge begins on the vi chord (Bm) and then moves to the emotional F♯7/C♯ chord, the V of Bm. If we've learned anything about Joel's bridges so far, it's that they are predictable in their unpredictability. This V chord resolves deceptively to a string of dominant chords before finally moving back to Bm and, lastly, toward the V (the G/A and A) of our tonic key of D.

Fig. 22

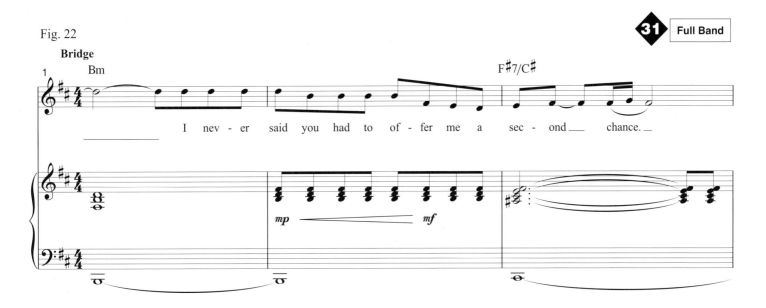

I nev - er said you had to of - fer me a sec - ond_ chance._

NEW YORK STATE OF MIND

Words and Music by Billy Joel
From the album *Turnstiles,* released in 1976.

Billy Joel is a New Yorker to the end, and with "New York State of Mind," he has written an unofficial anthem for NYC and its millions of citizens. In the song, Joel tells us that although he has traveled the country from coast to coast, there's no place like home. In fact, Joel is happy with any reminder of the city, such as the New York Times or the Daily News, and whether supping in Chinatown or driving down Riverside Drive, it's all fine with him. His performance of "New York State of Mind" at the September 11th Memorial Concert further cemented this song's symbolic resonance with the city.

Figure 23—Intro

"New York State of Mind" begins with an eight-measure intro in Joel's piano-bar style, played freely. Though he starts off clearly in C, he surprises us in measure 4 with the A♭maj7/B♭—basically a ♭VII chord borrowed from C minor. The rest of the intro outlines a ii–V movement, in which the F/G functions as the V.

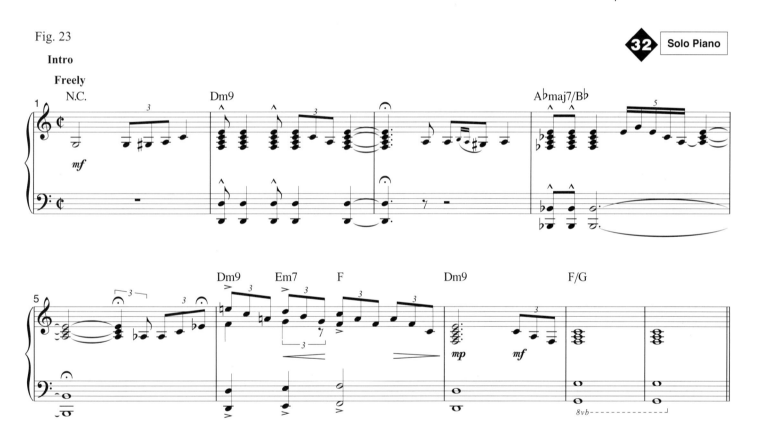

Figure 24—Instrumental Verse

This section acts as a second intro. Here Joel lays out the basic theme of the song: A beautiful, bluesy melody over what could be called an 18-bar blues. (Compare this progression to Ray Charles's "Hard Times.") Joel uses secondary dominants throughout, as many of the diatonic chords (Am, F, and Dm, for example) are preceded by their dominants (E7♯5, C7, and A7♯5, respectively). The B♭9 is the ♭VII chord (borrowed from C minor, and recalled from the intro); this chord contains the notes of an F minor chord (F A♭ C) and works great in sentimental settings like this one.

Fig. 24

 Solo Piano

Verse

Slow Blues (Half-time feel) ♩ = 60

Figure 25—Bridge

This bridge is the only real contrast to the eighteen-measure verses that abound in this song. Perhaps taking inspiration from the great Tin Pan Alley songwriters, Joel wisely avoids the compositional devices he used in the verse, both melodically and harmonically. The vocal line is broader rhythmically, yet falls in a tighter range. The chord progression is jazzier, with its frequent maj7 chords and wandering quality (moving from G to F to A, and back to G again before setting up another verse in C).

Fig. 25

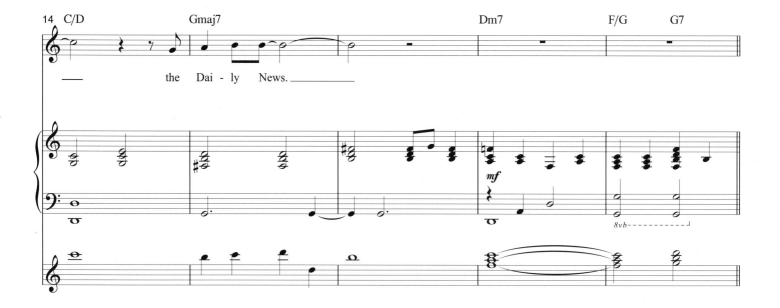

Figure 26—Outro

The outro presents a grand-sounding and dramatic close to an emotionally charged song. With held chords, solo flourishes, and wailing vocals, Joel sets up a fascinating ending. The final measures are filled with exciting harmonic twists, especially with the chords that follow the B♭9.

Earlier in the song, Joel resolved the B♭9 to C, but here (meas. 15–18) he resolves this secondary dominant to its I chord, E♭6, then follows with its IV chord, A♭, before jumping back to what amounts to a sophisticated and jazzy ii–V–I (C/D–D♭13♯11–D/C) progression in C. Basically, he is taking a trip around the circle of fifths leading back to the tonic: He moves from B♭ to E♭ to A♭, interrupts with the D, and then moves on to D♭, finally ending on C.

A further note on the final four measures: The C/D in measure 17 chord functions as a ii chord, followed by the D♭13♯11, which functions as V; jazz players call this the *tritone substitution*, because it is a tritone away from the V chord. The D/C is a colorful way to end; the notes of the D chord sound as the 9th, ♯11th, and 13th of the C chord.

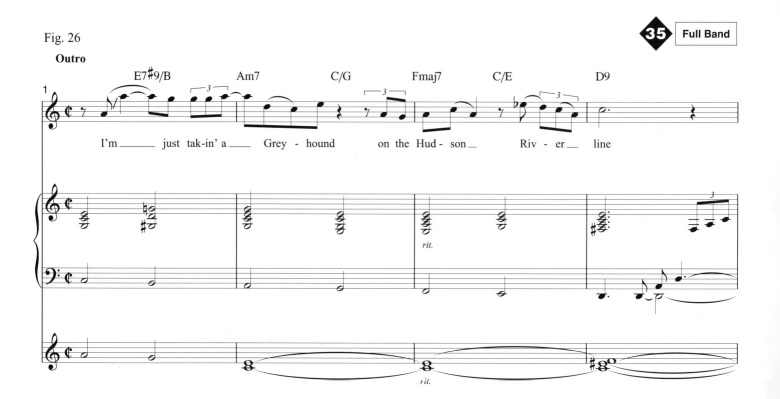

PIANO MAN

Words and Music by Billy Joel
From the album *Piano Man,* released in 1973.

"Piano Man" could be Billy Joel's signature song, a paean to barroom piano players everywhere and an enduring hit in the Joel pantheon. This "story song" features different characters and their intertwining lives, regulars at the neighborhood bar where Joel's piano man leads them through their favorite songs. From the opening line—"It's nine o'clock on a Saturday; the regular crowd shuffles in"—Joel sets the scenario of all these disparate people coming together to share in "a drink they call loneliness." He reminds us that "it's better than drinking alone," alluding to the sometimes-temporary camaraderie that drinkers create. It is Joel's title character who leads them in song and brings them together "to forget about life for awhile." Joel even gives the piano man (himself) hope when the regulars who "put bread in [his] jar" ask him, "Man, what are you doing here?" As Joel can attest, there can be a career in piano beyond the barroom.

Figure 27—Intro

The first two measures of "Piano Man" present a seemingly ad-libbed bit of riffing that adds to the song's piano-bar feel. The 4/4 time signature here is just a formality, as the section is meant to be played freely.

The main theme and verse progression start at measure 3, as the chords begin their descending waltz-style progression in 3/4 time. Instead of playing a straight "oom–pa–pa" waltz pattern here, Joel varies the duration of bass notes and chords subtly and adds interest while avoiding a cliché. The bass line descends straight down the C major scale for almost a full octave. Joel harmonizes this bassline with mostly primary triads (C, F, and G). The D7 chord at measure 9 is the first real surprise. The D7 serves as the V7 of V, and strengthens the movement to the V chord (G), which in turn resolves back to the root chord (C).

Measure 17 introduces the song's signature line, a repeating four-measure pattern with C arpeggios interspersed between chords.

Fig. 27

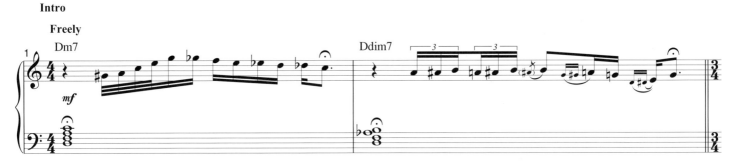

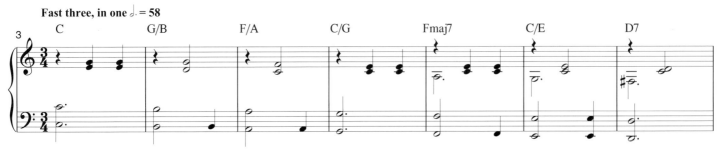

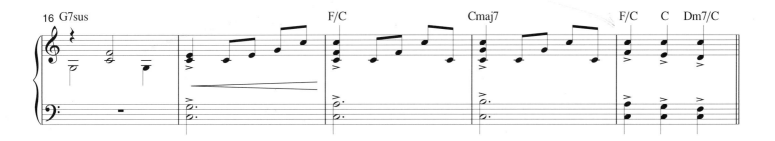

Figure 28—Verse 1 and Verse 2

The chords in the verse start out the same as the descending progression of the intro (now played in more of a straight-ahead waltz fashion to support the vocals), with the very small exception of a D in the seventh measure (instead of a D7). Joel then fleshes out his chords with some added 9ths and a G9sus chord in measures 13–14.

The two verses are separated by a brief harmonica interlude, played over a variation of the verse pattern, then the crescendo on C and F/C in measures 23–26, in which the accordion enters to add to the more rollicking second verse.

The chord progression in the second verse is essentially the same, but Joel's vocal melody soars an octave higher, registering great emotional impact. Notice the well-used G/B (meas. 42) acting as a conduit to the A minor chord that begins the interlude.

Fig. 28   **38** **Full Band**

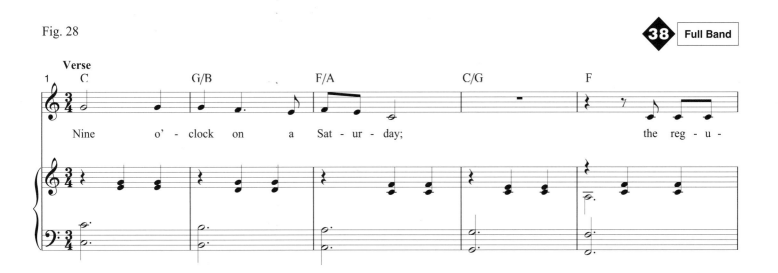

lar crowd shuf - fles in. There's an old man _____ sit - ting

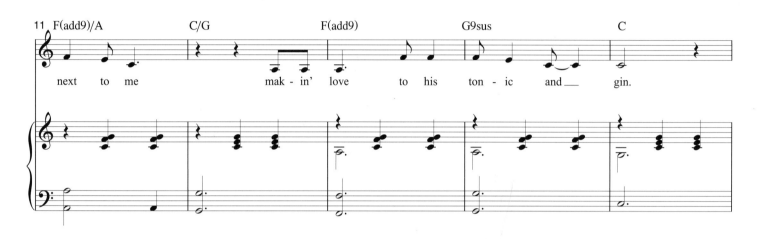

next to me mak - in' love to his ton - ic and ___ gin.

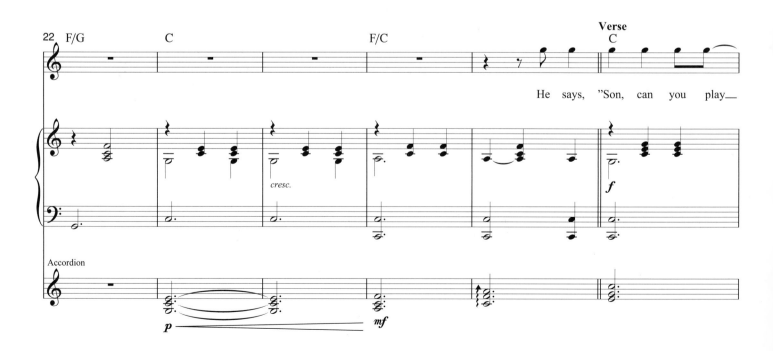

He says, "Son, can you play ___

me a mem-o-ry? I'm not real-ly sure _____ how it

goes, but it's sad and it's sweet and I knew it com - plete _____

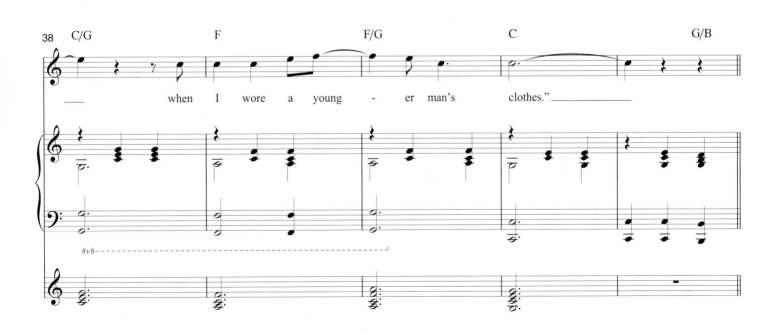

_____ when I wore a young - er man's clothes." _____

Figure 29—Interlude

The interlude serves as a transitional buildup to the sing-along chorus. Joel leads us down the A minor scale to F via a well-placed D/F♯ passing chord (meas. 3). However, the next time he uses it (meas. 7), instead of going to an F, he drops the bass note to make it a root position D major chord, the V of V, which he engages to resolve to the V chord (G). The last four measures of the interlude find our bass notes descending straight down the C major scale to the ultimate release of the tonic chord in the chorus. The overall effect is one big release of tension to the root chord of the chorus. Play the last four measures as a crescendo, building up intensity for the main hook.

Fig. 29

Figure 30—Piano Solo

The story continues through variations of chorus, interlude, verse, and interlude. Then Joel takes a piano solo over a progression similar to the interlude, ultimately setting up a big chorus before the last verse. The solo is constructed of strong lines primarily based on chord tones. Of particular interest is his bluesy playing over the D chord at measure 3 (the F–F♯) and the Am/G chord at measure 6 (the E–E♭–D).

Fig. 30

40 **Full Band**

Slow Demo: meas. 1-16

41

THE RIVER OF DREAMS

Words and Music by Billy Joel
From the album *The River of Dreams,* released in 1993.

The "River of Dreams" about which Billy Joel sings is equivalent to the stream of consciousness. The lyrics evoke all kinds of things; there are Biblical references, suggestions of baptism and resurrection, and a great deal of symbolism in the river and the seas. Rhythmically, the song is built on an engaging African-style drumbeat.

Notice the *swing sixteenths* marking after the tempo indication. This means that whenever you see sixteenth notes, they are to be played as swing sixteenths; that is, the second of each pair of sixteenth notes is played on the last *third* of a triplet, rather than on the midpoint between the two notes. In jazz, swing, and rock shuffles, there is always an underlying triplet feel. Make sure you understand the concept and feel of swing sixteenths.

The song features piano, Hammond organ, and synthesizer.

Figure 31 – Intro/Verse 1/Chorus/Verse 2/Interlude

After the opening drumbeat establishes the feel, the synthesizer with an "air choir" patch plays a syncopated chord sequence.

In the verse, the organ holds simple triads while the piano also plays fairly simple chord patterns. In the chorus, a synth using a flute pad is added. There is an interesting piano lick at measures 21 and 22. In the interlude, the piano becomes more rhythmically propulsive. Measures 36–39 introduce blues elements into the piano part, including the blue notes B♭ and F.

42 Full Band

43 Slow Demos
Synth meas. 1-4
Piano meas. 32-39

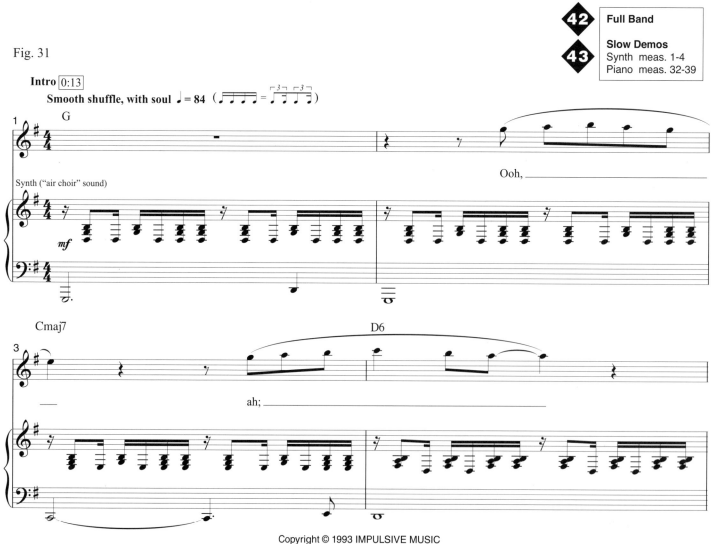

Fig. 31

that it can on-ly be seen _____ by the eyes of the blind, _____ in the mid - dle of the

night. _____

Interlude 2:04

ROOT BEER RAG

Music by Billy Joel
From the album *Streetlife Serenade,* released in 1974.

Billy Joel is best known for his pop and rock songs, but "Root Beer Rag" stands out as a rare instrumental. Joel created a credible ragtime piece that hearkens back to the days of Scott Joplin and James P. Johnson. "Root Beer Rag" is in the key of C major, and has a very clear and cohesive structure.

Figure 32—Intro and Theme

The intro is a two-measure pattern (the C–C/B–F/A–F progression) that is played twice. The eight-measure theme is somewhat repetitive as well. If we break the theme into two four-measure sections, we see the first two measures of each of those sections are the same, using the C, B♭, and F chords. However, the final two measures of the theme contain a unique progression, complete with secondary dominants. Here's a run down: The F (IV) moves to D/F♯ (V of V), which resolves deceptively to C/G (we expect G). Next, Joel emphasizes the D in the last measure by preceding it with its dominant, A7 (V7 of ii). The D as stated here has no 3rd, but later in the piece it contains an F♯, demonstrating that Joel treats it too as a *secondary dominant*—the V of V.

Fig. 32

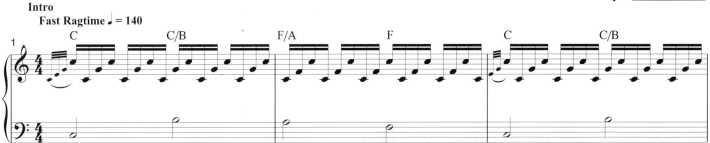

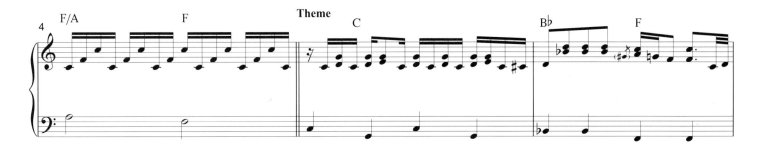

Figure 33—Variation

This eight-measure section is a variation of the original theme. Here Joel moves the right hand up an octave and adds some exciting rhythmic anticipations, as in the ends of measures 2, 4, and 6. As expected in a variation, the harmony remains virtually unchanged, and here the last two measures of the interlude are in fact very similar to the last two measures of theme, except that now the D/F♯ is clearly thought of as F♯dim7, and the D7–G7–C progression at the end is clearly delineated by fully articulated chords.

Fig. 33

46 Full Band

47 Slow Demo meas. 1-8

Figure 34—Secondary Theme and Interlude 1

The first eight bars of this section demonstrate Joel's understanding of harmonic logic and planning. On the surface, we hear beat-by-beat changes of harmony, filled with secondary dominants over a descending bass line. But if we listen more closely, the first part is a four-measure phrase in F, divisible into two independent *phrase fragments* (subdivisions of a phrase). These phrase fragments are linked by the C7 in measure 2. The first cadence on the tonic (F) occurs at the end of the second phrase fragment, in this case, at the end of the phrase itself. The next phrase (meas. 5–8) is a restatement of the previous phrase, but now transposed up and played in the tonic key, C. Joel continues in measure 9 with new material and a dramatic break before wrapping things up in measures 15–16.

Fig. 34

48 Full Band

49 Slow Demo: meas. 10-16

*Play lower notes w/.L.H.

Figure 35—Interlude 2

In this interlude section, Joel plays staccato *dyads* (two-note "chords") over a loosely implied dominant/tonic chord progression. In measure 4, he intensifies the texture by breaking up the basic pattern between the hands in a more syncopated fashion. Joel employs a chromatic descent in the chord progression, leading us down to an A7. The last two measures are true to the theme's harmony.

Fig. 35

 **Full Band**

Interlude

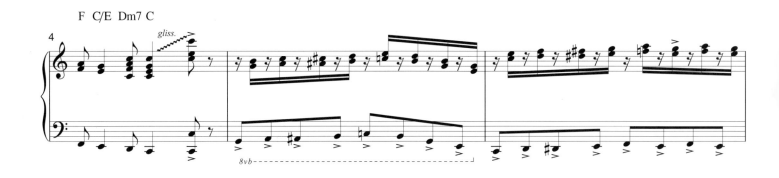

Figure 36—Bridge

This section in A minor, the relative minor of the tonic (C major), begins a typical minor progression over a descending bass line. Joel creates most of the musical interest here through his inventive but stylistically appropriate rhythms.

Fig. 36

51 Full Band

52 Slow Demo: meas. 10-12

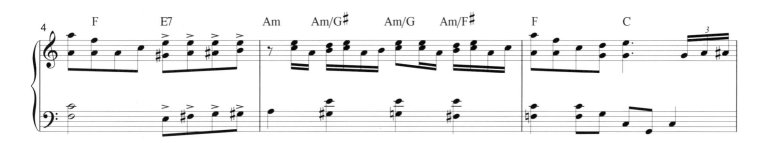

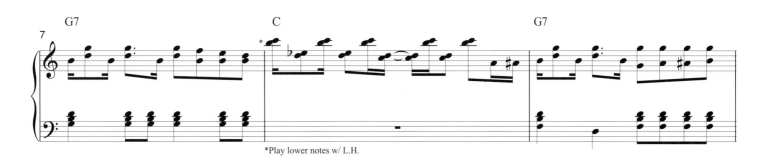

*Play lower notes w/ L.H.

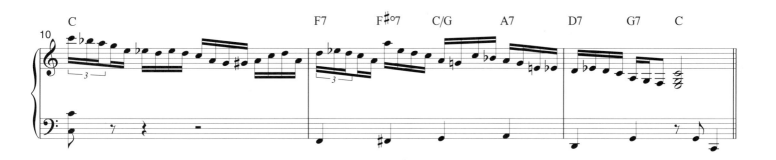

SCENES FROM AN ITALIAN RESTAURANT

Words and Music by Billy Joel
From the album *The Stranger,* released in 1977.

"Scenes from an Italian Restaurant" is one of Billy Joel's epic "story" songs, falling in line with "The Ballad of Billy The Kid" and "Miami 2017" as a multi-movement work using many characters and a stretching timeline. This song uses flashbacks to reminisce about the old neighborhood and the gang over a couple of bottles of wine at the Italian bistro in the title. Joel's vivid memories of his "sweet romantic teenage nights" lead to a vignette about Brenda and Eddie, the "popular steadies" whose changing lives are symbolic of their class and generation.

Figure 37—Intro and Verse 1

Joel introduces the song with simple chords in F. At the beginning of the verse, he helps establish the Italian restaurant vibe with the addition of an accordion sound. He continues comping on piano throughout and fills in between vocal phrases.

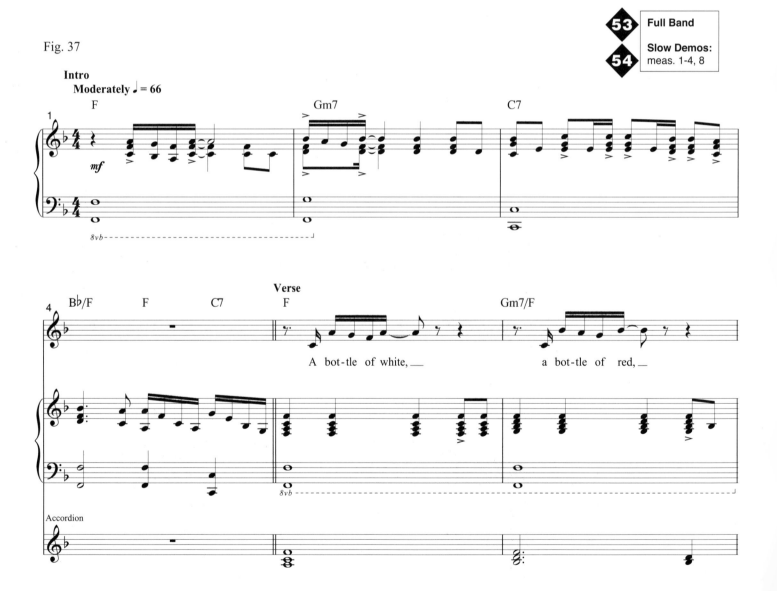

Figure 38—Piano Solo, Interlude, and Verse 4

The piano solo begins with a left-hand octave pattern in 16th notes. In measure 3, Joel plays some 32nd- and 16th-note flourishes. Listen to the solo demo of this first, and practice it slowly before attempting it at tempo.

Joel continues his 16th-note left-hand patter during the interlude and verse and adds syncopated chords in the right.

SHE'S ALWAYS A WOMAN

Words and Music by Billy Joel
From the album *The Stranger,* released in 1977.

In one of his most tender songs, Joel alternately praises and denounces the woman he loves. By using the ubiquitous "she" instead of a name, Joel writes allegorically of all women, and their effects on the men who love them. In the end he delivers the title sentiment, "but she's always a woman to me." The song sounds romantic, though a quick glance through the lyrics reveals the same disillusionment that other Joel songs like "Stiletto" deliver. "She's Always a Woman" is the polar opposite of the classic ballad "She's Got a Way" in Joel's canon. Ultimately, he takes the blame for all the things he lets her do to him.

Figure 39—Intro, Verse 1, and Verse 2

Don't let the changing time signatures of 12/8, 9/8, and 6/8 bother you—it's all to accommodate the melody, which has a very natural feel to it. The overall feel is always in three.

The combination of delicate chording, a smooth, flowing melody, and lyrical imagery makes the verses powerfully effective. Beginning in measure 9, note the gentle waves of arpeggios Joel lays down below the vocal as he builds into verse 2—a clear indication of his classical training—plus the addition of jazz master/Joel session-man Steve Khan's acoustic guitar in the second verse.

57 Full Band

58 Slow Demo
meas. 9-16

Fig. 39

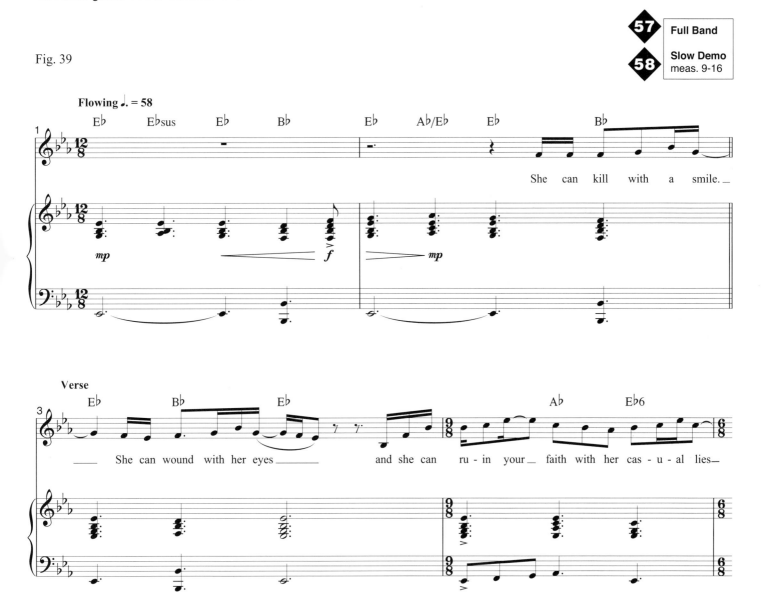

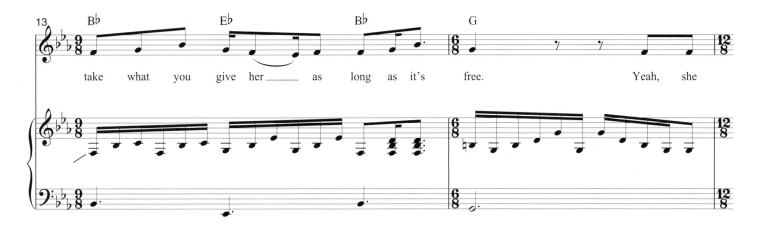

take what you give her ___ as long as it's free. Yeah, she

steals like a thief, _ but she's al - ways a wom - an ___ to me. ___

Figure 40—Bridge

The whole bridge is in 12/8 and begins on Cm, the vi chord, which helps delineate this as a new section. Billy sings at the top of his range to help contrast the bridge with verse. We also hear the familiar Joel device of stepwise, descending bass movement in nearly every measure. The arpeggiated style of playing established in verse 2 continues throughout the rest of the song.

Fig. 40

Bridge

59 Full Band

60 Slow Demo meas. 1-8

Oh, ___ she takes care of her-self. ___ She can wait if she ___

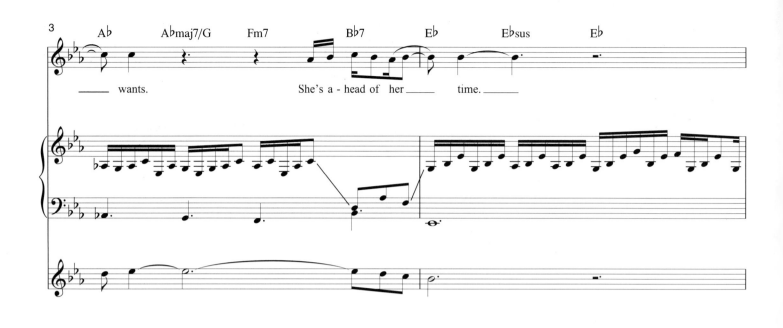

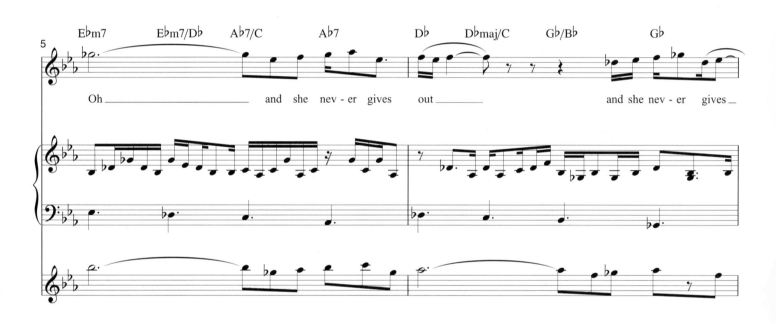

SHE'S GOT A WAY

Words and Music by Billy Joel
From the album *Cold Spring Harbor*, originally released in 1972, re-released in 1983.

This is one of Billy Joel's most gentle and effective ballads. He sings with an engaging emotional immediacy while he accompanies himself on the piano with simple but effective patterns.

Figure 41 – Intro/Verse 1/Verse 2/Bridge/Verse 3

The piano part consists primarily of triads played with the right hand (in the alto range) on each beat, while the left hand plays the bass roots in octaves in whole notes.

Each verse ends with a deceptive cadence. Instead of going to the I chord (i.e. G major) in measure 11, which is what the ear expects, the deceptive cadence inserts two extra chords between the V and I chords—♭VI (E♭maj7) and ♭VII (Fadd9). This style of deceptive cadence is considered standard in the cocktail piano repertoire and could be an influence from Joel's "Piano Man" days.

Fig. 41

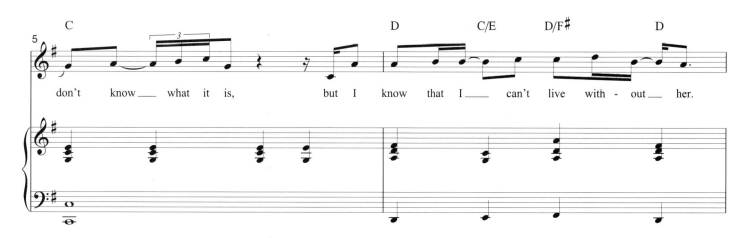

TELL HER ABOUT IT

Words and Music by Billy Joel
From the album *An Innocent Man,* released in 1983.

With its bouncy shuffle beat and tight horn section, "Tell Her About It" evokes the sound and feel of Motown girl groups of the 1960s, such as the Supremes or Martha and the Vandellas. The theme of the song is that you should always communicate openly to someone you're in love with, no matter how much discomfort it may bring.

Figure 42 – Intro/Verse/Chorus

The basic right-hand piano vamp features the alternation of triads in root position and 6th chords in a syncopated rhythm. The song changes key from B♭ to F at the chorus. Be sure to "swing" the sixteenth notes.

62 Full Band

63 Slow Demos
Piano   meas. 1-2,
14-17

Fig. 42

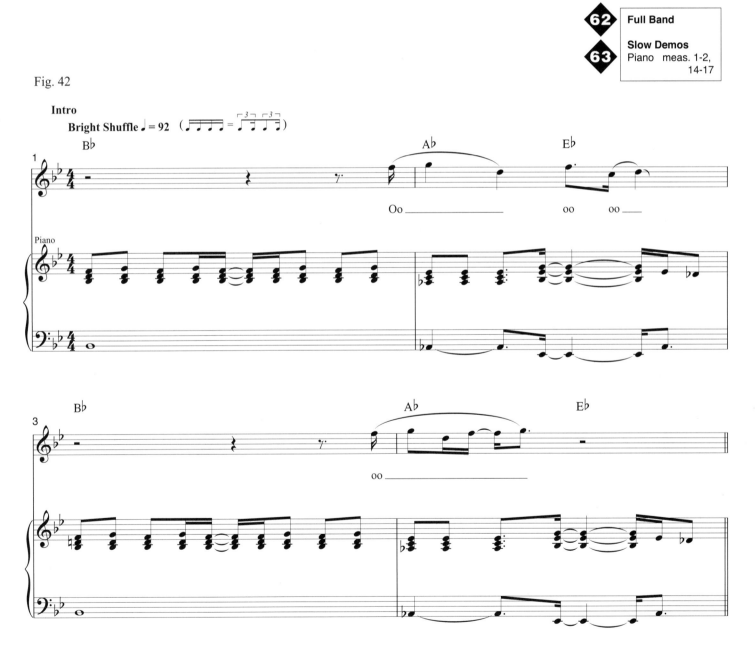

UPTOWN GIRL

Words and Music by Billy Joel
From the album *An Innocent Man,* released in 1983.

"Uptown Girl" evokes the high falsetto harmonies and bouncy beat of Frankie Valli and the Four Seasons, a group Joel loved as a kid. The song is sung by a "downtown man" for an "uptown girl," presumably Christie Brinkley (the supermodel Joel married in 1985).

Figure 43 – Intro/Chorus/Verse/Chorus

The main piano part consists of simple triads in the right hand played on each beat, with the left hand playing the bass notes in a slightly syncopated rhythm. The harmony is built on an ascending bass line: E–F#m–E/G#–A–B7.

At the verse, the song changes key from E to C, but the piano pattern remains the same rhythmically.

Fig. 43

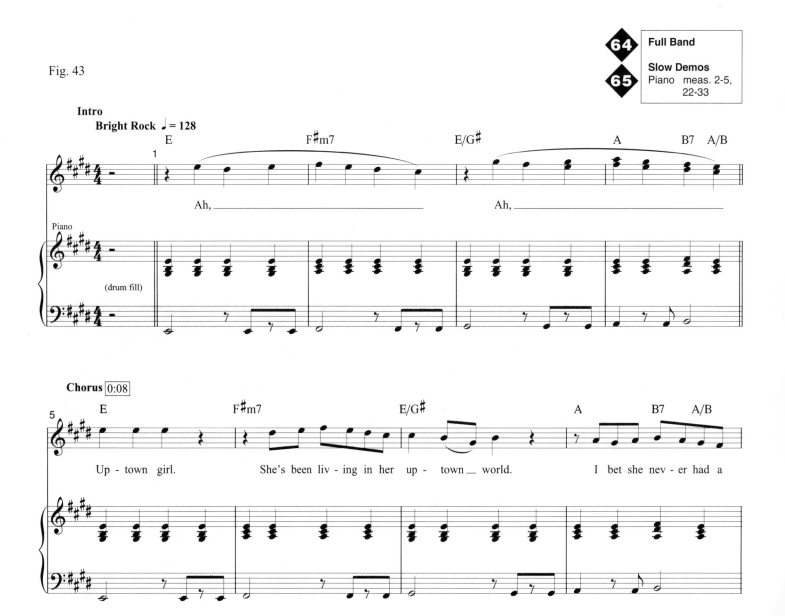

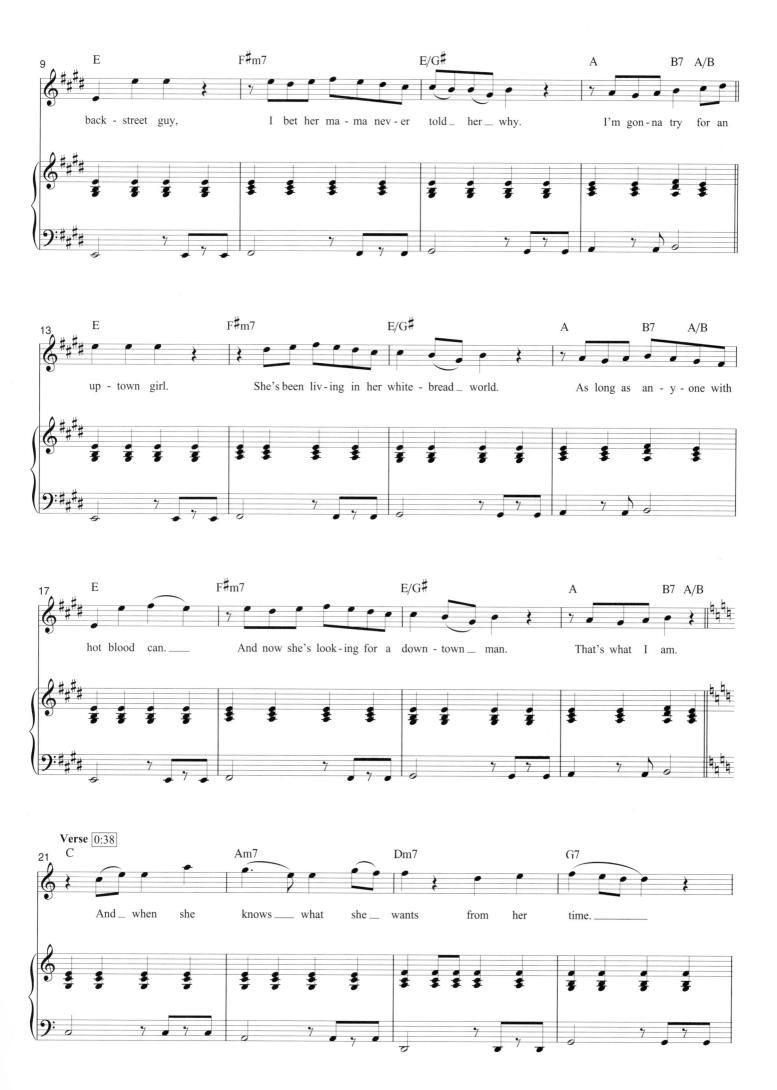